75691

LET'S
see

The Bald Eagle

by Pamela Dell

Content Adviser: Kelly Sorenson, Executive Director,
Ventana Wilderness Society, Salinas, California

Reading Adviser: Dr. Linda D. Labbo, Department of Reading Education,
College of Education, The University of Georgia

Let's See Library
Compass Point Books
Minneapolis, Minnesota

Compass Point Books
3109 West 50th Street, #115
Minneapolis, MN 55410

Visit Compass Point Books on the Internet at *www.compasspointbooks.com* or e-mail your
request to *custserv@compasspointbooks.com*

On the cover: A bald eagle

Photographs ©: Creatas, cover; Photo Network/Mark Newman, 4, 16; Digital Stock, 6, 18; Bruce
Coleman Inc./Gail Shumway, 8; Bettmann/Corbis, 10; N. Carter/North Wind Picture Archives, 12;
Tom Brakefield/Corbis, 14; Tom Stack & Associates/Thomas Kitchin, 20.

Editor: Catherine Neitge
Photo Researcher: Marcie C. Spence
Designers/Page Production: Melissa Kes and Jaime Martens/Les Tranby

Library of Congress Cataloging-in-Publication Data
Dell, Pamela.
   The bald eagle / by Pamela Dell.
       p. cm. — (Let's see)
Includes bibliographical references and index.
Contents: What is a bald eagle?—Is the bald eagle really bald?—How did the bald eagle become America's
national bird?—What is the Great Seal?—Where else does the bald eagle symbol appear?—Did everyone want
the bald eagle as America's national bird?—Where do bald eagles live in the wild?—Are there many bald
eagles in America?—Is the bald eagle safe now?
ISBN 0-7565-0616-6
1. United States—Seal—Juvenile literature. 2. Bald eagle—United States—Juvenile literature. 3. Emblems,
National—United States—Juvenile literature. 4. Animals—Symbolic aspects—Juvenile literature. [1. United
States—Seal. 2. Bald eagle. 3. Eagles. 4. Signs and symbols.] I. Title. II. Series.
   CD5610.D37 2004
   929.9—dc22   2003014455

Table of Contents

NOTE: In this book, words that are defined in the glossary
are in **bold** the first time they appear in the text.

What Is a Bald Eagle?

The bald eagle is a large, powerful bird that lives only in North America. It is also an important symbol for citizens of the United States.

The bald eagle has a fierce, proud appearance. It is easy to recognize because of its white head and sharp golden eyes. When its wings are spread open, they measure about 6.5 to 8 feet (2 to 2.5 meters) from the tip of one wing to the other. This length is greater than the height of most basketball players!

Bald eagles are found in every state except Hawaii. They are also found in Canada. There are more of them in Alaska than anywhere else on Earth.

◄ *About half of the world's bald eagles live in Alaska.*

Is the Bald Eagle Really Bald?

Bald eagles are not **bald!** The word *balde* was once used by English-speaking people to mean "white." The bald eagle is the only eagle that has a white head and a dark body. This is how the bald eagle got its name.

Young bald eagles are all brown. A few feathers may be white or lightly streaked with white. Their heads and tails begin to turn all white at around four or five years of age. Bald eagles have feathers all over their bodies, except on their lower legs.

◄ *The bald eagle has a white head and a dark body.*

How Did the Bald Eagle Become the National Bird?

American colonists fought the Revolutionary War (1775–1783) to gain their freedom from Great Britain. Winning that struggle made the new Americans feel proud. They wanted a symbol that showed the pride, power, and freedom of their new country.

The bald eagle had a proud, powerful appearance. It sailed high in the air, **soaring** free. Most of the new nation's leaders wanted this proud bird as the symbol for the United States. In 1782, they included the bald eagle in an important design called the Great Seal.

◀ *The bald eagle symbolizes the freedom of the United States.*

What Is the Great Seal?

The Great Seal is one of the most important symbols for the United States. It shows in pictures and words what the country means to its people.

The Great Seal is often shown in public. It hangs behind the president when he gives an important speech. It is printed on the president's stationery. It is a powerful symbol of the nation and its president, and it is recognized all over the world.

The Great Seal is the most important place that the bald eagle symbol can be found.

◄ The Great Seal is a powerful symbol of the United States.

Where Does the Bald Eagle Symbol Appear?

The eagle has appeared in American designs since the early days of the country. Bald eagles have been pictured more than any other kind of eagle. They can be seen on many different types of objects, old and new.

When it is shown as a symbol for the United States, the bald eagle is most often seen on money and flags. It appears on old gold pieces, modern coins, and dollar bills. It can be seen on the flags of many states. Bald eagles also appear in designs used by the American military.

◄ *The bald eagle appears on the presidential seal at the Franklin Delano Roosevelt Memorial in Washington, D.C.*

Did Everyone Approve of the Bald Eagle?

Benjamin Franklin was one of the Founding Fathers of the United States. He did not want the bald eagle as the national bird.

Bald eagles often steal food from other birds. They are sometimes chased by smaller birds. Franklin thought the bald eagle was dishonest and lazy. He also did not like choosing a bird that seemed so afraid of smaller birds. Franklin thought the national bird should be the turkey.

For many years, the country's leaders fought angrily about what to do. Finally, in 1789, they chose the bald eagle as the national bird.

◄ Benjamin Franklin wanted the turkey as the national bird.

Where Do Bald Eagles Live in the Wild?

Bald eagles rarely live near people. They usually live in lonely places, far from large cities and towns. They make their homes near rivers, lakes, and other large bodies of water. They build huge nests in the tops of tall, old trees. Sometimes they nest high on rocky cliffs. They eat mainly fish and small waterbirds. They sail in the sky for hours looking for food.

People love to watch bald eagles in their natural surroundings. Every year, people gather to watch large groups of bald eagles in the wild.

◄ *Bald eagles live near large bodies of water.*

Are There Many Bald Eagles in the United States?

There have always been thousands of bald eagles in Alaska. Once, there were almost as many in the lower 48 states. Human behavior has hurt the eagles, however. There are not as many as before.

As cities grew, the eagles had less wild land to live in. Many eagles were hunted and killed. Also, people sprayed poison to kill insects. The poison got into the lakes and rivers. Then the poison passed into the eagles' bodies when they ate fish.

By the 1970s, many Americans feared that the bald eagle would soon be gone forever. It was put on a special list of animals that needed protection.

◄ *Much has been done since the 1970s to save the bald eagle.*

Is the Bald Eagle Safe Now?

In the 1960s, there were fewer than 1,000 bald eagles in the United States. By 1998, that number had grown to more than 11,000. Many people have been working hard to help the bald eagle.

Scientists study the birds to find out more about them. They watch where the eagles fly and **breed.** This helps them understand how to keep the eagles safe. Scientists help injured eagles get well.

Important laws have been passed to protect the bald eagle. No one may hurt or kill a bald eagle.

These protections are important. With them, the beautiful national bird will never disappear from North America.

◀ *Scientists find ways to make sure the young bald eagles survive.*

Glossary

bald—having no hair on the head
breed—to produce offspring by hatching

soaring—moving through the sky on the air without moving wings

Did You Know?

- Once a pair of bald eagles nest together, they stay together for the rest of their lives.

- Bald eagles are safer now than they once were. In 1995, they were taken off the list of animals that are in danger of disappearing forever. They are still on another list, though, because they are not yet totally safe.

- Bald eagles have excellent vision. They can see a mouse running on the ground from a distance that would equal about eight city blocks.

- The huge nests that bald eagles build are called eyries.

- Old Abe was a famous bald eagle. He was the mascot of some Wisconsin soldiers during the Civil War (1861–1865). Old Abe lived through nearly 40 battles. After the war, he was taken home to Wisconsin, where he lived for many years.

- There is a story in the country of Wales that says brave warriors flew to heaven by taking the shape of eagles.

- Native Americans can ask the federal government for bald eagle feathers for special ceremonies. No one else may have these feathers.

Want to Know More?

In the Library

Binns, Tristan Boyer. *The Bald Eagle.*
    Barrington, Ill.: The Heinemann Library, 2001.
Gibbons, Gail. *Soaring with the Wind: The*
    Bald Eagle. New York: William Morrow
    & Company, 1998.
Morrison, Gordon. *Bald Eagle.* Boston:
    Houghton Mifflin, 1998.

On the Web

For more information on *bald eagles,* use
FactHound to track down Web sites related
to this book.

1. Go to *www.compasspointbooks.*
   com/facthound
2. Type in this book ID: 0756506166
3. Click on the *Fetch It* button.

Your trusty FactHound will fetch the best
Web sites for you!

Through the Mail

American Bald Eagle Foundation
P.O. Box 49, 113 Haines Highway
Haines, Alaska 99827
info@baldeagles.org
To receive information on the largest
gathering of bald eagles in the world

On the Road

Montezuma National Wildlife Refuge
3395 Route 5 & 20 East
Seneca Falls, NY 13148
315/568-5987
To see bald eagles nesting in the wild

National Zoo
3001 Connecticut Ave. N.W.
Washington, DC 20008
202/673-4717
To visit a refuge designed especially for
bald eagles hurt in the wild

Index

About the Author

Pamela Dell was born in Idaho, grew up in Chicago, and now lives in Southern California. She began her professional career writing for adults and started writing for children about 12 years ago. Since then she has published fiction and nonfiction books, written numerous magazine articles, and created award-winning interactive multimedia. Among many other things, Pamela loves technology, the Internet, books, movies, curious people, and cats, especially black cats.